WAKING
THE BONES

WAKING
THE BONES

MELISSA
MYLCHREEST

THE DOROTHY BRUNSMAN POETRY PRIZE
BEAR STAR PRESS
COHASSET, CALIFORNIA

WAKING THE BONES © 2014 BY MELISSA MYLCHREEST

Printed in the United States of America on archival paper.

10   9   8   7   6   5   4   3   2   1

Direct inquiries to the publisher:
BEAR STAR PRESS
185 Hollow Oak Drive
Cohasset, California 95973
530.891.0360 /bearstarpress.com

Cover art: Matazo Kayama
(A good-faith but ultimately fruitless
effort was made to find the holder of rights to this work.)
Book design: Beth Spencer
Author photograph: Craig Rigdon

The typeface for the book is Adobe Caslon Pro.

ISBN: 978-0-9850584-5-6
Library of Congress Control Number: 2014935005

The publisher would like to thank Dorothy Brunsman
for her support of the press since its inception.

Acknowledgments

Many of these poems were included in a chapbook, *Reckon*,
which won the Merriam-Frontier award in 2011.

Under a different title, "Across the Street, the Midwife Arrives" won the
2008 Dorothy Sargent Rosenburg Prize for Poetry and was featured on their
website.

"The Gap-Tooth Girl" won the 2011 Obsidian Prize for Poetry and was
published in *High Desert Journal* Issue 14.

"For Jolene" won the 2012 Obsidian Prize for Poetry and was published in
High Desert Journal Issue 16.

"Frenchtown" and "July, Montana" were published in *Crab Orchard Review*
Volume 18, Number 2.

Thanks:

To Dorothy Brunsman, who made the publication of this book possible.
To the poets, writers, and artists who have encouraged and inspired me,
including Charles Hartman, Judy Blunt, Joanna Klink, David Moore, Greg
Pape, Erika Fredrickson, Chris Dombrowksi, Lee and Amy Secrest, Andy
Seguin, Joy French, Jeff Medley, my MFA cohort at the University of
Montana, and the Naked Ladies — Grace, Lindsay, Beth and Britta.
To Mom, Dad, Gramma, Papa, and the rest of the family who have supported
and loved me in my wandering and wayfinding.
To Craig and the menagerie, for their constancy.
And finally, to Montana and the New England coast, the unparalleled places
that gave rise to so many of these poems.

Contents

Family, friends: This is for you.

ACROSS THE STREET, THE MIDWIFE ARRIVES

For what it's worth,
Spanish has no verb
"to give birth."
             Instead,
mothers *dan a luz*, give, after
so many months in the growing dark
their burdens to the light.
             Why are we made
to forget the brightness breaking,
the enormous world suddenly rent
into existence?
             Would we be too eager
in our remembering, rush towards
the next unexpected
on the other side?
             Or would each dawn's heft of being be
too great without the light's
surprising palm beneath us, lifting us again?

DRIVING THE EASTSIDE HIGHWAY TO THREEMILE

Cows outside Corvallis, bridges of hipbone
and skin spanning dust to dust. The late afternoon

wind pours from the mountains and runs
between their legs like a sweet-clear river.

The road dances in the heat, unctuous flood
of tar and grit. Every few miles, deer

carcasses swell in the ditch, salsify and knapweed
cradling them. On the rise, that house still

stands, half-built and left, canted corral
of sun-warped plywood and Tyvek

like a pale flag. Every splinter here
a story. Every well pecked and post-hole

augured along a stubborn sighting.
How our habits cling to the rightness

of angles, the hem-stitched
edge against fraying fields, the long straws

of industry siphoning and shuttling
water above the ground. The men

spend days doing nothing but moving
metal to coax alfalfa from the rock.

Down across that draw, the paths of three
paint horses braid together

like an old prayer. Once the youngest
followed me to hay each morning,

and I'd stand close in the thin light, for the heat,
the sharp dark smell of him, the truth

of so much muscle and blood. What earthly good
is it to believe in horseflesh? Or the meadowlark's

flagrant voice? And yet we stall
in dawn chores or in the dirt road's ruts,

our breathing quieted. That great heart. The bright
bell of the throat opening and opening,

song like a gate-hinge loosed, a break
in the fenceline, a trail coiling back into the hills.

FRENCHTOWN

They shutter the mill and still the mill
stink settles in this valley, and men
soured — thirty years of a sure thing
and now this shame — turn to their old friends
and then the bottle and for a few
there's finally the certain comfort
of blued steel. Once the great trucks groaned
and downshifted up to the gates all day.
Amid steam and noise, a kind of coarse
brotherhood: lives gathering trucks, wives,
high school football and the Frenchtown bar.
So one morning at the hardware store,
what honor's left in *Tom, we've been friends
twenty years. Can you give me a job?*
Tell me, what else can a man do,
that pulp smell dogging him like a ghost?
And one day the *Missoulian* runs
a three-inch mention and everyone knows
the newsprint is trucked from Canada
where trees still fall and a good man can die
in his traces if he chooses.

Almanac

I.

Measure the months
by rain, faltering sun,
the mountains' downdraft marking
the ebb and flow of days. All around us
the drumbeat of hours. All
of our ends come. Against it
we go on anyway.
In the in-between,
.tiny gods forgotten and listening.
A run of coho. A tree
scarred for cambium.
The way our hands conjure fire.
Alchemy of rivers and earth.

II.

What of the way the mind folds
back on itself? When the light in the hills
brings you elsewhere, who do you become?
Surely there is more to us.
Yesterday, the cranes gathered
the evening beneath their wings
and rode over the valley,
the string of them like the body
of a snake, their going an old
and holy thing.

III.

There were stories long before words.
Fish litter the banks and their stink
climbs back up the rain. From everywhere
out of the forest a congregation
of fur and mouths, blood in the river's
teeth, the trees' hundred hungry tongues.

IV.

In the night the great bear comes, stands
before the cabin and listens
to the hunter dreaming. The snow
comes hard from the north. Reverence is
quietly standing everywhere:
In the morning,
tracks all around the fire pit, tracks
melted deep before the door.

V.

In spring, boulders rumble
in the runoff like a great herd.
The body resonates with
everything around it.
At night we lie on the earth to feel
their thunder in our chests and above us
an arc of animals lights the sky.

VI.

When out of the darkness you imagine
a humming, a great
breathing, the sound of a hundred wings,
the sound of silt polishing stones,
what you are hearing are
instructions.

VII.

Even if nothing matters:
This morning, fifteen ravens
over the gulch, talking. This morning,
a hawk alighting in pines. Fog
in the creekbed and horse
silhouettes on the ridge. Breath
condensed and the heart working
loudly on the hills.

THE GAP-TOOTH GIRL

The gap-tooth girl is dancing, and the man
in Wranglers holds his arms around her like
a loose hoop of rope, a snare for her tight
two-step. The band will never play better
than this town limits, and still it's sweeter
than the sounds the country makes, gumbo mud,
trains coupling, a wild Chinook, a place laced
with ice and barb-wire singing. Her hips have
land in them, are good enough for dancing
but in those jeans look ready-made to sit
a horse all day; she wears the weather in
her hair. How easily the bar-light shames
our faces sallow and city-broke,
but she blooms like some wild prairie weed.

Men bled sod and themselves for whatever
it is glowing in her and never found it,
dug in worn boot heels until their bodies
gave out in this place where nothing rots
but bones and barns dry up and blow or burn
away. This whiskey is a myth and why
I'm here. We are those men. A woman
with cat's eyes turns and turns before the dark
pedal-steel player like a fence-caught feather
in a gale. The night wheels. The gap-tooth girl
is dancing all alone, the tin band moans,
the wind outside is making blizzard songs,
and the West shakes off this game of lost or won.

FOR JOLENE

b. December 10, 2010, Pablo, MT

Scrap, small leaving of a night and its wild biology,
      hound bodies unfenced and wrought-up, sly coupling
of the junkyard, car a rusted crib, weed-bound hulk of comfort for
      one, two, three, and then
you, mewling mess of kinked ears and blood, pink pads, the echo
      of a million years in your bones. Winter-born you were
stubborn for life's sake, nested with your brothers, suckling hard
      milk from just a pup herself, rag of the reservation.
The world opened around you and your body began:
      let me want, and let want be only a kind of joy-to-be.
Dawn riser, marionette of no one, you run
      for specters — the herd, the hunt — for the sheer
grand hell of it, for sleep swift and deep, for the toothsome
      treasures of the field you'll dig to your haunches
and for coolness, a crater in the willows. Half-breed, halved
      and halved again until what are you but entirely
yourself, willful beguiler, what else but dog clear through?
      Watchful and stubborn still, remnants of that thin beginning
and the savvy of genes, what grace bred in us both
      brings you to my hand? Marrow-memory
of the cold so close. Shared breath warning off the dark.

Eight Days and Eight Prospects:
from 46.88 N, 114.01 W & 2.20.11 – 2.27.11

2.20, E

Blizzard's limbing the Siberian
elm and the wind's on a clattering
errand: it's a battlefield out there, the
Visigoths've got nothing on this, night
of Arctic knights errant and eastern
ire galloping through Hell's Gate.

2.21, NNE

In some languages that make these distinctions,
trains take the animate form of the verb. They mumble
and thunder today past the house. Empire's dromedary, pack
of pack horses, skein of elephants made
of coal and timber. I watch sleek airplane bodies
nose east through the fog, whale parade on wheels.

2.22, WNW

These are the northern lights or they're
cirrus clouds high and writhing for the moon
like a harem. Sidereal seduction, how can we resist
running out to eye and ahh, ground glowing
around our boot prints and the town asleep? *So much*,
they say, *is unknown*, roiling their hips and the stars
dazzle like a thousand bright bells.

2.23, S

Sometimes time reveals itself; light
and snow conspiring sketch the edge
of the Holocene, right before our eyes —
shorelines scoured in the South Hills and a valley
filled with fog: a dozen millennia gone and we're alive
on the lake bottom. This soot's
a new silt, we're the ebb and fill.

2.24, W

Last summer's swiss chard incorrigible, it has dug
itself out, unkinked and reaching
in the watery light. Little wonder, such talk
of resurrection all the world over; whatever
has been worth our faith but this, again and again:
the world unneedful of us to go on?

2.25, S

The Sapphires put on the evening like a gown.
They remember there's something worth
dancing about, coming later, smelling
like apples and fresh trout and mud.
Around the hem, restless herds, and here
and there scarlet accents where first calves

kick and breathe. The mountains catch up
a tuft of squall, powder their shoulders.

2.26, SW

Sunlight like an opera today; tremulous
extravagance raging and ranging
but in the end poorly spent, this town
unversed in the language and tin-eyed
to the gestures of clouds, profligate
as some confectioned soprano.

2.27, NNE

The end nearing, crows worry
last fall's dregs out of snow, and in pairs
carve updraft edges over the north
hills. Wing-roll and sideslip,
dance of hollowness and keratin.
The one gimp of them made it through
winter totters and shakes
his balled claw at us from the fence.

Adelaide

I want a dog with whiskey-colored eyes, she said. I want
a riot of light in the morning, a sliver
of mercury above zero, a sky that rips me
apart each day. Give me, she said,
an indifferent god keeping score in the shadows.

Out here, a shutter tries its luck on the wind. The sun's
bleached linen, dilute liquor, dry sourdough, color of
nothing. When the wheat fails the houses
come undone. This kitchen holds a table still, seed
catalog painted with birdshit and mouse-torn, the floorboards
canted hard back to earth. Curtains as fladry at the windows
warn us away like the wolves we are. Dry grass and gate hinge
make a spare hymn over the land and nothing holds it,
horizon a fiction toward which all things run. Black birds
circle cottonwoods and an upturned washtub thumps
like a heart, wind-rocked in the hedgerow. This home's
history breathes and trembles at the center, twitches
and eyes us circling. We stand in the yard
in our liminal and only bones.

Adelaide, could it have ended any other way, marked
as you were? Beneath that tallgrass, an aquifer
curdled and dry. Beneath a thousand stretched wings
a nightmare of flightlessness. A body deviled. You were the teacup
in that kitchen years ago, carefully gathering flies and pollen, making
treasure of dust, until one day the walls just gave out. A sudden sky
so unending and lovely you went to pieces in the dirt.

ECLIPSE

Forgetting is not like
not remembering: seeing all
the small stars of having loved you
blink out to black
is like lying
on a grave, calling
into the bones of the earth:
"Memory, have you
no cold space there
for me?"

BITTERROOT AND SWEETGRASS

I.

You arrive out of the weather
smelling of bar oil and fir, and bending
to your bootlaces drop a snow
of splinters and leaves. Cutting firewood
all day high on Moccasin Ridge, you saw
a horse loose in the mountains. You shake
rain from your shoulders and I wonder
what hard and honest hope frees a pony to the hills
rather than keeps it wasting, slack-eyed in the valley,
what kind chance waits away from fences.
The kitchen radio says the market's fallen, bombs, the sky is
closer now than ever, and though I say *hello, I love you, there's*
stew, what I mean is: handle me, like you handle
that saw for hours, let me snort and buck.
Halterless and skittish, it watched you
from a clearing and turned to your voice,
came nearly to you. Then it spooked
like an elk, turned untamed, running
between lives.

II.

I have not planted asparagus in the garden
and for this I blame you. Two summers of faith
and fine weather needed to make the work worthwhile,
such permanence: sow the crowns, salt the soil,
wreck the ground forever after. Once you're in
you're in, and it's *points d'amour* for good. How could I
begin, unsure as I was? Who's to say we'll share
anything after so long — two years! — this plot, these
green suppers and ineluctable days, the way we parry
the future. Four springs ago we made no
promises and kept them. We've believed we are
our own. But just now you've come up to this bed
time's made ours, thousand-night arena of everything
that holds us, socks and towels
our own evidence, animals that know us
as theirs, even all these books keeping company
in the corners. How much do we need? Better
a bet than a barren tract of weeds and doubt.
Our sleep no longer wakes each other.
Adventitious heart-work of years, we're dug in
despite ourselves, small knot of roots set and holding.

III.

You first held me in the shadow
of the mountain, eyes foxfire
and an atavistic hunger
festering below your ribs. I came
an offering, slim wrists and hank
of hair plaited to my waist, moon-skin
and the blue scent of snow. In your palm
talons of an owl nested like twin mice,
and you ran those severed bits, down
and needle-point, along my cheek.
I can't say I didn't bargain for you, for this
kettleful of flesh and whims, ragged
want and those days of silence worse than
blizzard-wind, can't pretend I never knew
when I opened the door, said
animal, come in.

DEAR HELEN

I remember arriving that day you were canning rhubarb; you ran out into the white sunlight waving a dishrag, the screen door banging. In the kitchen, bright lids bounced in the bottom of a pot, tossed copper light around the room. You had cut daffodils stuck in a cup, a watercolor of a nautilus half finished at the table. Later, we rocked on the porch talking and listening for the lids to pop themselves tight, pouring tea, then gin, to drink neat from jam jars. I held mine curled against my chest, watched you watch the wind on the bay, and the sun rested on your face as it does on something familiar; the slope of shale running to shore, the sweet beeches, the flank of North Mountain gone red too. When we fell silent, the space hummed with thick light, the sea burned as though made of tinder, and swallows rode the bright beams of air, their flight the shape of laughter over the lupines. I understand now the sadness in you that I could not have seen then, all those years ago. I saw only what I admired: a solitary woman rooted to that sea-hemmed mountain, your painterly hands and the deep creases at your eyes. Not the nights and winters long with ghosts and doubt, the emptiness of your rooms. I was running for no reason, hadn't learned how we come to hold so tightly what little we have. Now I see. Now my face creases, too. We spend our days building bulwarks against loneliness, the smallest objects and events of our lives a kind of frail armor. The inexhaustible palette of the sun, the slender pink-armed rhubarb, those shoddy hinges and the warm gin. The inexorable days. Those mountain hours and slim suppers by the stove, a print of Rothko by the door. I see now they were yours, and inadequate, and enough.

CREATURE

I.

You, rumpler of life's road,
like winter's freezing architecture
of dirt you came and heaved,

>   your need decades old,
>   half-orphaned and running
>   like a hell-bent horse

>   you'll never break.

II.

My body a basin
for licking clean,
>   what could I do
>   but lay a pallet on the floor
>   and feed you?

III.

You made a life
of naming all the birds.

You wanted a bird, slim
shock of feathers to dance

and go and roost again,
like the not-quite-pet
crow demanding
nothing from the trees.

I wanted the mist-net:
fingers and breath,
the delicate panic of capture,

the warmth of captor's
hand, the metal bands.

I learned to mimic flight
for you, the lightnesses
of indifference.

IV.

You'll never break: go on,
show the crushed bones
of your hand, the place your
muscle shrieked loose and curled
on itself like a wave. And tell it
like nothing.

Go on: say
my ministries
are untenable,
you, man-child,
you, soul-stunned.
Fatherlost.

V.

I will swaddle you in feathers.

I will pluck and stitch
the makings of a blanket.

VI.

Come:
      I will unhand you
      to your galloping

      if you
      tell me again the story
      of your emptiness.

            Hold yourself
            to the blunt light.
            Is there hollowness and ice? If you find
                none of it

      show me again
      if you can

      the workings
         of a wing

      muscled machine of more
      and less —

            tell me how we cannot fly
              without a hole
                 breaking
            open above us.

July, Montana

Twenty-seven days
over 100 and on every one a fire,
the summer turned so hot the trees went to ash.
    There was no sky that month
but that close, still pall,
and when late some days the sun showed
like a dull blood orange in the west I stood
in the slow streets to stare. Nights, purple
lightning, green heat keeping to the hills.
    One midnight we wrestled
your mattress to the front room for the open door,
for the air when it moved, waking early
into a precious cool hour
from dreams that smelled of smoke.
    Sweatstain, parched skin, the salt
stain on my tongue from your skin, it was a season of taste
and absence. No rain.
Before and after helicopters, silence. Before
and after love, silence. No stars. No telling
the time, no need beyond our three rooms on 3rd,
the market on Orange Street. Nothing on the walk back
but the road and the charged air
watching the progress of a bag of peaches
and limes, *arancia sangue* Italian ice
that would melt before home.
    We fed each other
ruby spoonfuls, a sharp, sour
supper to cut the haze, drank long
after dark, naked at the kitchen table, glasses
dripping the night's only constellations
to burn and burn off our thighs.

CALLISTO

She-bear, mother of Arcadia, mother
of wilderness, bringer of breath
in the darkness. Raven-watched, stone-
coated, color of high water, color
of the widest pines, platter-faced and
-pawed, your every cell
rain and high wind, stormlight
and clover. How long is your
memory? When the ice came,
you wrung a life from the coastlines,
salmon and seal, and when the ice left,
you let the mountains swallow you
in winter. You are short-grass, you are
scree and sinew and know nothing
less than each inch of this
valley. How many times have you
lain just so, here at river's edge,
quietly breathing in the light? The evening
gathers itself around you, aligned,
your place here as right as stars.
Callisto, I am stumbled-footed
before you, arrived suddenly as I am
out of the willows. A small bird
awakens to you, batters
its wings within my ribs, reaches
for you with its every wild part.

HEARING THE BEATLES IN LAKOTA

At AmVets, off-key voices
cut above the smoke and din
and the bartender pedals
karaoke like it's the next
big thing. When I sit
the man at the end of the bar
leans to me — Hey,
who wrote this song? And I
tell him John Lennon.

That's right. He was
pretty good, he says.
That one song, Imagine. I
liked that one. He's
dead, right?

Ross tells me he's from
Pine Ridge, away east
of here.

I used to
speak the language,
he says, but now
I don't know. What
do I know? I'm just
a crazy old Indian.

He hollers for
the bartender, Hey
Georgia Peach! And calls
for a round for us two.
He holds one aloft, holds
one hand out to me.

Wanehāke, he says. It's what
I have always said,
wanehāke, one more between
friends, because you
and me, we are, and
John Lennon, too.

WANDERING IN CHERRY GULCH

On this morning's walk, the dog practices
pouncing, springing out of the ditchweeds

foxlike, feet pulled tight against her belly
and landing nose-and-forepaws-first, once,

twice, again and again vaulting through
dry grass, drawn by mice

or deer spoor or even
grasshoppers, lazy at this late date.

A mile farther down the path, a dead vole,
deflated scrap of fur she sidesteps, pays no mind.

There are days I want to start it all
all over again, be sent back to the beginning

like in the game of Chutes and Ladders,
sliding on that slick turn of fate

back to origins, scoured and
fertile. I remember one summer

when I felt I had nothing left
to lose. Alone and uprooted

I had never been happier,
spent the long daylight reading

Li Po and T'ao Ch'ien, believing
there is nothing but mountains

and rivers, wine and the blue-green
kingfisher watching from the shore.

A hermitage and a broom.
And maybe that's all there is.

This path is what I've got, flanked as it is
with knapweed and burrs, a handful of

worn stones. But it continues, and I
continue. Cottonwood and aspen. Above,

ravens and cirrus. Isn't this day its own
newness? The dog goes on

with her bounding, and I think I should
join her, learn her tricks, because

isn't this just how it goes? Leaping again
and again into the darkness, feeling before us

for a taste of warmth, for the sudden
fluttering heart of anything?

Ranging to the limit of this morning's
joy, it isn't tomorrow I'm looking for.

American History

I.

They string along the length of the world's spine.
They are the darkness moving within
cutbank's shadow, moon over Egg Mountain,
the ragged memory of thunder
roiling from a coulee like a gift.

II.

Once there was a right way
to tell stories: once the earth unhanded itself and gave
the makings of a world. It cracked open, a seed,
and we began. Crow watched, blue sheen in the pine and an eye
like a bead, our tottering progress. We rooted as animals. Once the rain broke
its own ground, once we died at its knees. We bent our claws to iron
and dug a runnel in the sand, made a rank noise in our throat
like the churning of a great herd. Once Crow thought
well enough of us.

III.

They ran a thousand miles
through winter and the sureness of capture.
They unfurled their sashes in the dirt and through them
thrust an arrow, pinning them to earth
and enemy's pounding approach.

They are the sudden flight of smoke,
the hank of rattler wound in a ditch.
Rime, duff, wind-rider, the red-rock spires

like sentries by the banks.
When they run it is like a vision
you have not quite seen: a frayed
disturbance in the distance, a glancing
echo in the hills. They are a
trick of the light, they are
a bright chanting in the aspens.

IV.

Once there was a sky chiming and open
like a bell, once there was a map of high white
blooms through the hills. Crow marks the dark robes
coming like a storm from the east. Once they believed
there was no end, and once the land crawled
under a tide of fever.

V.

They are making themselves
known. When we climb back into
the mountains, we wear the winter
like an ice-furred cloak they have
sent us. We will never be warm.

On the riverbank, willows rise
from their powdered bones. We drink.
The sky wakes in a chorus of eyes.

VI.

Crow watches. We clatter together
like scree, shards loosed and wracked, we grind
ourselves to dust. Our words bicker in the chamfered corners
of stories. Once we touched the ground. Once we knew flesh
as flesh, now carve ourselves to totems of raw want. Crow passes
a wing before the sun. The rain begins to leave.

VII.

We go to our knees in the dirt, our arms flung like rags to the high clouds:
It was not us! Arch-god, tracker of beginnings and ends, believe!

They are the susurrus of air. They ride out to circle
the storm around us, the plains snapping. They've cracked
for the marrow of bigger beasts. We feel the ghost of flint at our throats.

VIII.

When we go down to the earth
they will greet us, their arms already
in the shape of our bodies.
They have always been waiting.

The shortgrass wears itself out, gasping and selvageless into the rocks.
They are here. Look. They rattle the blades like a wind.

SELIN IN THE DESERT

after Gregg

Selin the days retreating the days a train
of horses roiling into nights the desert
desolate starguarded Selin of unkempt days.

In the dust in the stars Selin running
horses to the hills for nights for keeps
Selin guarding for foxeyes like stars running

in the dust. Days of sage Selin for you
a hillside of fox-fur retreating the wind the
wind of horses canyoneer desert keepers

of night-flanks slick and star-dappled
Selin. Running to sagedust to horse-time
your days to unkept nights spark of fox

in the canyon Selin desolation keeper
of horsetrains rolling desert watcher
your nights starlit windridden fox-marked.

Animal

We stand shoulder to shoulder
around the cutting table, muscle and tendons
a kind of grace laid before us. A body comes to pieces

under our hands. Around our feet, dogs, and on a pile of blankets
a baby girl asleep. Our voices and laughter weave
a net around us as the dark comes down the mountain

and the other deer appear again at meadow's rim.
Two sisters were baptized into wilderness, two
handfuls of glacier-melt the holiest water I know.

In the spring, bears will spill out of these hills and
call up the clover. The rain will follow, the river.
Ravens will sharpen their beaks on these bones

and the same jays' calls will rattle down the pines.
This infant sleeping beneath butchery was made
from meat, slick red fibers built of snow and grass.

She is mineral and iron. Under the moon, circling a fire,
her blood will remember stories, and beyond the edge of the light
she will know we are animal. Someday we will be earth

again, someday this blade will go to rust, handle wracked and gray.
But our teeth are white and fine in the dim light,
and tonight there is nothing else but this, the careful work

of atoms and the ready business of the heart,
counting *now* and *now* into the dark.

Lexicon for Survivance

This is the sign of the dead.

This is the sign for "give me."

This is the sign of the pox, who goes and what comes after.

This is the sign in the ledger book for "there is no one left."

This is the sign of the Black Robes, a new kind of magic.

This is the sign of the blood of the lamb, marking a kind of mercy. They said. They said.

This is the sign of *unshika*.

This was the sign for mercy.

This is the sign of what we will take.

This is the sign of your name: X.

These are the signs for your new name: S-A-R-A-H. W-I-L-L-I-A-M.

This is the sign of a burn in her palm that turned her Saint and saved her.

This is the sign for white man: nih'óó3oo.

This is the sign for spider: nih'óó3oo.

This is the sign for gold in the hills.

This is the sign for "give up and take up this hoe."

This is the sign for wagons and guns.

This is the sign for unspeakable.

This is the sign for escape, a chart of stars and need.

This is the sign for calling up death: the white hand.

This is the sign I make on my horse.

This is the sign I make on my truck.

This is the sign of Wovoka.

This and this are the sign of the Sun Dance.

This is the sign of the dog-tooth bite.

This is the sign of the Dog Soldier.

This is the sign of the basketball star.

This is the sign for language.

This is the sign of what remains.

This is the sign for "feel my child kick."

STORYTELLER

In a cave in Spain they have dug up
compassion. Bones grew wrongly
half a million years ago but he lived
long, longer than biology imagined.

This not quite man, spine-bent
Homo heidelbergensis, couldn't hunt
or carry, could only, it seemed, lean
on a staff and hope.

But why care for such a creature?
What's of any worth beyond stone and spear,
butchery, the opening of bones, a cave for staving
off the night?

They found in his kind, too,
the first ears built for fine hearing, the cause
or effect of language. Imagine he cobbled
stories for his keep.

When he died a pit was dug.
Cast over his body, they say, were
red ochre and new words, protection
for the journey and the genesis of prayer.

ASPIRARE

I.

The bellows will creak at the hinge, slow commerce of time
and so much unlit, and I begin to doubt my chance for fire.
I re-pile the tinder, I tighten. A machine for breathing,
lifeless twigs at the hearth, mantel, stage of prettiness
beneath which nothing burns.

II.

Archipelago of promises, flung across the years like Cassiopeia's
joints unfurled across the sky. She lashed her daughter
to the rocks, sea-soaked virgin squirming on the headlands, salvage
for Perseus, blood up, fresh from slaying the wrong-minded, childless
gorgon. Shame. Shear the head that countermands the body.

III.

When I made my mother a rind,
when they hauled me from that brackish bath, who's to say
it was anything like benediction?
I had all my chances even then, a bowlful of jilted pearls
and the anatomy for flight.

IV.

Yeast-bread. Soup of sustenance. I am a homemaker
again and again, a cup, a crop, each rehearsal a spectacle of selflessness,
action and reaction only possible: gathered
pebble on the shore, the arm cocked, kettle-pond still slick and nervous,
no rings yet run from a flung stone. Nothing hatched or shattered.

V.

In fever dreams, I misplace the orphan infant at every turn,
somber and want-eyed creature without words or origin, slippery
changeling appeared in my arms and asking. You are furred
with your newness, make a fist like an invention.
I will not lose you.

VI.

Fractus heart of two minds, how to decipher leech
and love, the body brandishing and the world's wants
a stockroute over me? I'm more than loam. All the workings
of my hands, are they less than the making
of the smallest fingerbone?

CHART

Purl:

   Dawn   song,

sibilant
  choir   of whelks

       and stone throats breathing.

Architecture of salt
  and time: How long a thimble?
       A castle?   Daily this island

enclave of drift-oak and ground   whale bones

      arrives and goes. Sieved bits.   Sidereal
          siphon,   marionette of the full pearl moon.

Live here: Know the cadence of water as a pulse,

 reckon yourself by the voices in your blood.

        What else a mudflat but a map of hours?
          An anchor a compass for minutes?

Count by clam   and salt marsh haying,

 brackish ice, the almanac

of wrack line.   One sea year:

    An exhalation.

Wave's erasure
        of its own
  sighing
     self.

GHAZAL

Somewhere dream-borne, these muscles ache to fly over the ocean
shuddering under sudden pinions, high over the ocean.

Where have I gone, sweet sea left behind like the best old lover?
Adrift in such high, tideless land, I cry over the ocean.

Here there are sometimes gulls winging oddly among the rooftops,
pirouettes lacking the damp air to ply over the ocean.

Such a timeless dance, the parrying of jealous paramours:
The earth and moon know forever they'll vie over the ocean.

Elsewhere a kestrel rides the wind above salt roses and dunes;
rise and fall, she makes the shape of a sigh over the ocean.

A day will come when nothing can keep me. Friends will ask "What's this?
Where are you going?" And I'll say "Goodbye. Over the ocean."

Association

I.

You unsettle me
the way the submarines shipping out
unsettle me,
have crept beneath cover of dark
under my skin,
sounding secretly places unseen.

II.

I left you sleeping
to stand
naked on the lawn
the night we first made love,
watched the sky weep
Perseids
burning down to earth.
The moon was empty,
the Pleiades
pale old women
with no sympathy,
and in the dark
the water churned out solid shadows,
lazy bullets through the night.

Jekyll Island

The birds mew and moan. Beyond the peacock house she harbors. Dim glade of live oaks shawled in moss, murmuring like crones over the dead. Out on Jekyll Bay, wind gathering and still the thin clamor of wind chimes from the porches. Ruffled confections of women "oh!" and clutch their upset petticoats, hats aloft. They flee mallets and wickets to squeal through the gale indoors. Her eyes are the color of seas. She wears a ribbon in her hair. She climbs an oak to watch the water dance. Spindrift. The waves crest and lose themselves. She rides the crown, the ribbon whipping. Away in the shallows, a brig flounders. The peacock cows and the peahen howls. Away at the house, shingles clatter, a shutter pounds itself free. When she was born, her mother saw her sea-bound eyes and fell into a sickness. When she died, the nursemaid took the girl and taught her. The brig breaks. She wears a beacon in her hair. She keens and the musk of Cherokee rose rises like a haint. Up from the waters she wills the past, pale and want-eyed. The sailors will shriek and go down. In the glade she'll uncorset herself to the touch of a wraith, to crest and lose herself. The gale hammers. The ladies will cower alone.

I Dream of Neruda and His Weariness

I dream of Neruda and his weariness
standing side by side, two old men
in the barnyard, a mess

of chickens around their feet
chasing grasshoppers, stopping to peer
up with their belittling small eyes.

I wait within a grove of trees for them
to see me, in the grass beneath, or above
among the leaves, languishing

on a limb, my thighs almond-
colored, my hair hanging down
like a shadow in the wind.

One begins to speak to me —
Estoy cansado ... — but the other
takes him by the arm, *No, vámonos, Pablo,*

and I must come out of the trees
to watch them go, down the road past
Tocopilla that will take them to the sea.

VIEWING THE SCULPTURES AT STORM KING

At Storm King strolling among legs
of metal giants, the day hot
early but from the city you brought
a thermos of cool tea, your bag

a rucksack worn and full of taste;
asparagus, sheaf of poems,
film camera. How odd we both
wore straw hats, how our promenade

is a portrait of history,
I in my blue dress and you your
linen, the Hudson-heavy air
touching like a tongue backs of knees

and neck. Our long correspondence
anachronistic, how fitting
to fetch you at the train, waiting
months for this short, chaste dalliance:

art and talk. It is August. We
sweat into our mint tea to taste
salt. Once, we knew something of grace,
this field a stage for reverie

and the improbable, stark faith
in man and man's idolatry
of beauty. Elsewhere there's plenty
of hurry. Sit down. Why erase

each moment's shape almost as it's
arrived? I've come a continent
to see you. Look; steel represents
there, wind, and elsewhere, staid patience.

Imagine the paths of letters
a kind of sculpture, monument
to time and space, an insistent
arc of ponderings unfettered

as the geese that wing and settle
all day between the two small lakes.
I'll not see you again. The brakes
will pant, train head for the trestle,

metal making for departure,
so be still, lie here and leave your
shape in the grass by mine. The hour's
ours, the art. Let us not squander.

SIXTEEN ANSWERS FOR THE MESSENGER

I. VIA

And if the road ends there is no end.

And if the moon wanes, so let it
be enough for wayfinding.

What of the arrow through
the hart's throat? What of these
hounds at my side, hungry?
They roll their whited eyes,
paw the earth, their baying
rattles the oaks.

We run the river-edge, our twinned
images shadowing every step,
the jealous water
at our feet like tongues.

II. Cauda Draconis

So it goes. So they chase their tails.

It is best to stop before it begins, but who
am I to interfere?

Here in my cup, a little spell for
scattering. Here in my left hand, lantern-light
like the truth of truths. I let them fall
where they may.

Come, bird. A little blood
for my troubles. Let us send our
greetings to the king.

III. Puer

A sword is itself and it is everything
like it. Cities go to their knees and their women
swell in his wake. He imagines himself
godlike. *Alala!* on his lips in conquest like the first
primal syllables.

A vengeful and ancient sky grows weary
of his ways, double-faced and everywhere aflame.

Bane. Wrong-headed,
whisper the voices around him
as he falls.

IV. FORTUNA MINOR

Milkweed.
Foxglove.
The quick and shifty ways
of magic in the bones. Luck
like light from the sky. How death
rattles its way up the spine like
a sudden wind.

I tend my flocks. I am fit in muscle
and mind, and when I sing
these voices are not my own.

Look. See how the clouds
part, how the fire
is never still?

V. Puella

She says,
> *I am the ragdoll*
> *of the gods.*

She says,
> *yes–no–yes.*

She arches her back
and quivers, a strung bow, dress
falling around her like water. Her skin so white
he believes he can see her blood
running in her veins thin as air. Hers
is an atavistic act. All around her,
the scent of pollen and salt.

In his dream she opens to him
like a thousand welcoming mouths.

VI. Amissio

I will be like honey
on your tongue.

Myrtle and rose,
rushes and mint.
Imagine that I
walked out of the sea
for you. Imagine
that. Empty for me
these jars of wine,
before you turn your head.

Venenum, venenum.

Oh, tincture.
Oh, how we break
and go down.

VII. Carcer

We never falter, never
fail the fire's tending.

We mix emmer and salts
then move through the streets
ugly and untouched. We come with
finest wool. Who knows but us
the favored palate of the
gods? Milk and wine,
the ashes of the unborn
calf. Without us, a city
in ruins.

Mola, Immolare.

How brightly we burn.
How callused our knees.
Never mind these
shackles, never mind
these ropes and chains.

VIII. LAETITIA

Come up from the sea,
my horses, let me see
how fine you are!

Over the land, a thousand
hooves make the sound
of a great river. Dappled
and roan, they are multitudinous
as fishes in the shoals.

All of my animals well, my
bride comes to me here
between earth and sky.
I see her as though through
a dark and shifting light, pearls
dazzling like stars at her throat.
Within her, a son quietly swims.

IX. Caput Draconis

And so it begins.

The shadow of a great wing passes
over the moon, and all around me, black
birds awaiting divination.

I am the anvil and the agony
of iron. Do you hear how my arm
sings? My word is good as this
good earth you stand on, good
as bread.

Far off, thunder holds
court in the hills. Cover yourself, child,
before I glance your way.

X. Conjunctio

Borders and luck.
Trickery and thieves.

Come down the road to meet me,
let us dirty our backs in the weeds.

I promise:
All around us the fields
trembling and alive.
Our beautiful children will be
invisible.

See the way my body devours
itself for you? See how you swell
like corn after rain?

I say,
look how the new day breaks.

I say,
serpents and wings.

Vervactor, Insitor, Messor, Conditor.

XI. Acquisito

She comes up into
the hills for it,
belly a stone.
Fire in her hips and thighs,
the branches alive with
auspices. She wears the dawn
like a lavish quilt while she moans.

In the dirt two newlings
kick, their eyes bright
and the color of mountains.

The world below awaits augury.
She turns their faces
to the sun,

Now,
she says.

They open their mouths,
fill their lungs with sky.

XII. Rubeus

Come, my love,
he says.

Do not be afraid,

eyes pale as milk
and fingers itching.

How the pulse flutters
like a snared bird. How the blade
is rusted at the edges. Within the
woodlot, there is no one
to hear. All around, fur and
mouths, red trails in snow.
The underbrush shelters
a hundred worshipful eyes.

Oh, my disobedient brides,
he says.

How the bodies
twist and rise.

XIII. Fortuna Major

The ancients fought
when you were born
to keep you
on the other side.
I came with my leaves
and bones and coaxed you
into the light.

Look, enough: Your cheeks
are red and smooth, and the sun
comes north again.
Let us have wine and song.

What else?
A kind and pious sister
at your side.
A fierce and ready
drumming in your ribs.

XIV. Albus

Follow me, twin.

Place each foot in each
foot carefully
through the sand.

Around us, land like
a broad bowl.
Around us, light
so bright it sings.

Nimbus-headed,
they say. Oracular.
What do you think,
brother?

Here, water from a stone,
and a cup to catch it in. Drink.
Let us wet and cool our shoulders
before we lead the dead
back home.

XV. Tristitia

Handmaid of grief,
she moves with the
mournfulness of water,
wraps herself in linen
to walk in the orchard
of souls. How to choose?

Beneath her feet the
industry of decay. A hundred
stones crack around
the years.

Over and over
the ripe fruits fall.
Over and over
she recites the litany
of their names.

XVI. Populus

The least animal.

How they shuffle and
bleat, how they follow.
Soft and frail under the
hard moon, how can we
but pity?

Scritch, scritch,
go the talons on the roof.

So much clamor, so much
pounding of chests.
Their faces rise to us.
How quick the wave
is coming up the valley,
how quick the wave
is come.

Miraculum

It is morning. These animal
bodies of ours are waking
into their each and ordinary
ills — knot in the back, dim
eyes peering to the window
for weather. These tottering pyres
of blood and habit, what
inelegance! Outlandish
flaps and lids, runnels and
tufts, how unlikely the whole
machine. But, we could do
worse — nematode, effete
bird of paradise, harp
seal like a mustachioed
cigar — and body says only *I know*
what I know when asked how
life works, so we don't, and we carry
on: if there's coffee there's
coffee, and we believe the day's
doable. There is a dog that needs
out and a cat underfoot and feet
that ferry us obediently over
floorboards, a hundred years ago
nailed down by another body
got up by the sun, set and
wound like a watch cog, whirring
and pounding away.

NOTES

WANDERING AT CHERRY GULCH

The italicized lines are from T'ao Ch'ien, "Wandering at Oblique Creek," as translated by David Hinton.

LEXICON FOR SURVIVANCE

The neologism "survivance" was coined by Anishinaabe scholar Gerald Vizenor, a combination of "survival" and "resistance," suggesting that for native peoples, the act of survival is an act of resistance.

"Unshika" is a Lakota word that roughly translates to "pitiful" or "pitiable," a person in need of mercy.

In the Arapaho language, the word "nih'óó3oo" means both "spider" and "white man."

SIXTEEN ANSWERS FOR THE MESSENGER

Each of the sixteen sections is based on the characteristics of one of the geomantic figures used in the ancient practice of geomancy, or earth-based divination.

About the Author

Melissa Mylchreest was born in Simsbury, Connecticut, and moved to Montana in 2006. She earned an MFA in Creative Writing (poetry and nonfiction) from the University of Montana, as well as an MS in Environmental Studies. In addition to the Brunsman prize, she has received the 2012 Merriam-Frontier Award for writing, a 2008 Dorothy Sargent Rosenberg Prize for Poetry, the Obsidian Prize for Poetry in both 2011 and 2012 from *High Desert Journal*, and a residency at the Hall Farm Arts Center. She lives in Missoula.